Those Excellent Eagles

Jan Lee Wicker

Illustrated by Steve Weaver

Photographs by H. G. Moore III

Pineapple Press, Inc.
Sarasota, Florida

Inquiries should be addressed to:

Pineapple Press, Inc.
P.O. Box 3889
Sarasota, Florida 34230

www.pineapplepress.com

Library of Congress Cataloging-in-Publication Data

Wicker, Jan Lee, 1953-
Those excellent eagles / Jan Lee Wicker.-- 1st ed.
p. cm.
ISBN-13: 978-1-56164-355-4 (pbk. : alk. paper)
ISBN-10: 1-56164-355-6 (pbk. : alk. paper)
ISBN-13: 978-1-56164-360-8
ISBN-10: 1-56164-355-6
1.   Eagles--Juvenile literature.   I. Title.
QL696.F32W53 2006
598.9'42--dc22

2005032300

First Edition
10 9 8 7 6 5 4 3 2 1

Design by Steve Weaver
Printed in China

To my husband and best friend, Chris Wicker,
who soars on wings like eagles.

Contents

Why is the American Bald Eagle our country's national bird?

The eagle reminds us of strength, courage, and freedom. When choosing a national symbol, Americans felt these were important. Benjamin Franklin thought the wild turkey (also a native bird) was a better choice. He felt the eagle was not a good choice because it eats carrion (dead animals). Aren't you glad the turkey didn't win?

EAGLES
RULE!
TURKEYS
DROOL!

Why is it called the Bald Eagle?

It is not because its head is bald as in "hairless." The name "bald" comes from the old English word "balde," which means "white." It is a white-headed eagle. A young or immature Bald Eagle has a dark head and tail. The head and tail don't turn white until the eagle is about 4–6 years old.

Do all eagles look the same?

No. There are 4 groups of eagles. The harpy eagles are the first group. Some of these very large birds are 41 inches tall and weigh 20 pounds. The large fish and sea eagles are the second group. The Bald Eagle is in this group. The medium-size snake eagles are the third group. The booted or hawk eagles are the last group. They are called booted because of the feathers on their legs, and they come in all sizes. The golden eagle is in this group. There are varieties of color, patterns, and size in each of these 4 groups.

1. Harpy Eagle
2. Bald Eagle
3. Crested Serpent Eagle
4. Golden Eagle

Where in the world do eagles live?

The large harpy eagles live from Mexico to Brazil and in the Philippines. The snake eagles live in Europe, Asia, and Africa. The booted eagles live in Europe, Asia, Africa, and North America. The fish and sea eagles live all over the world except South America. The Bald Eagle is in this group, but it only lives in North America. It lives near big lakes and rivers in Canada and the United States.

Bald Eagle

Hawk

Turkey
Vulture

Osprey

Golden Eagle

How can you tell the difference between an eagle and other birds of prey when you see them flying?

Their profiles when they fly look different. Has anyone ever drawn your profile? Sometimes you can recognize someone just by looking at his or her profile. If you look up into the sky and see a bird that looks like a wave then it's a hawk. The Bald Eagle looks like a straight line when he flies. The osprey looks like an m. The common turkey vulture's profile looks like a sharp V. The golden eagle's profile is a wider V.

How do eagles protect their eyes?

To protect their eyes, eagles have a bony area that hangs over their eyes. It shades their eyes from the sun so they can see into the water better. They also have 3 eyelids. They have an upper and lower eyelid like we do and an extra eyelid that opens from the side. This lid protects and cleans the eye. Eagles can see in color. This helps them recognize their prey (an animal hunted by another animal for food).

What unusual things does an eagle do?

An eagle can turn its head backwards (like the one in this photo) to see behind. Our neck muscles only let us turn our heads from side to side. An eagle can even turn its head all the way upside down. Eagles can also swim. They use both wings like a paddle. It looks a lot like a swimmer doing the butterfly stroke.

SWIM TEAM

What do eagles eat?

The American Bald Eagle eats fish as well as carrion (dead animals). Other eagles eat ducks, rabbits, rodents (like mice and rats), frogs, snails, and snakes. The largest eagle, the harpy eagle, eats monkeys, parrots, and sloths. Eagles eat about 1 pound of food a day.

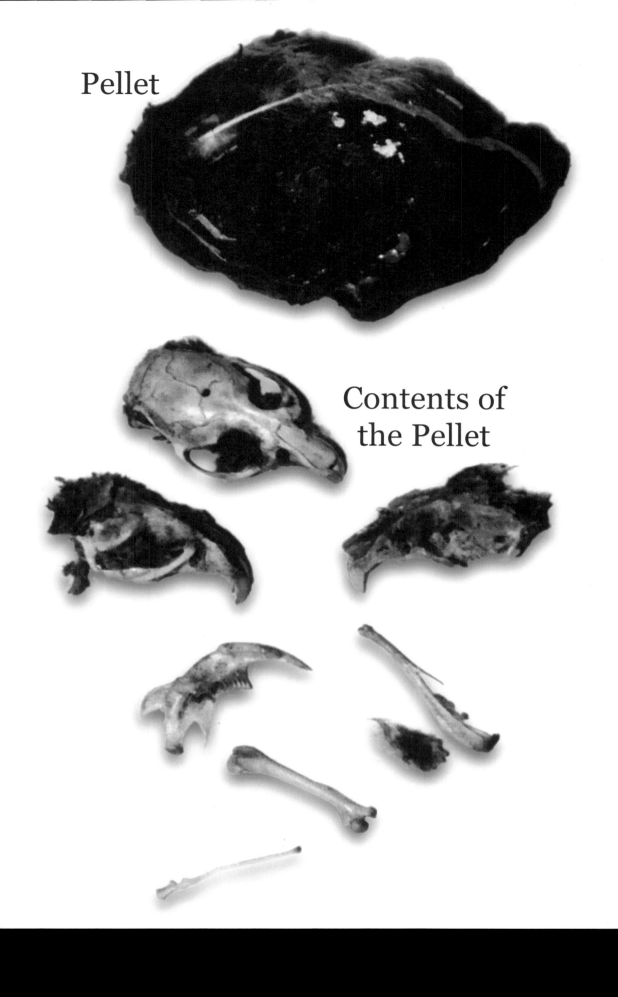

Pellet

Contents of
the Pellet

How do eagles digest bones?

Eagles have an organ called a gizzard that keeps the food they can't digest. Things such as feathers, teeth, bones, and fur form into a pellet. Then the eagle can spit it out. This is like a cat spitting out a hair ball after it licks its fur for a long time.

Are eagles' wings used for anything besides flying?

Eagles can cover their babies with their wings to protect them from the rain. This is called "mantling." Sometimes an eagle will mantle or cover its food with its wings to let other animals know to stay away.

How strong are eagles?

Eagles are the strongest birds in the world. They can fly while holding onto animals that weigh as much as they do. An eagle's grip is so strong that when it grabs its prey, its prey dies right away.

Harpy eagles have the largest talons (claws). Their talons are 3 inches long. The Bald Eagle's talons are 1 ¾ inches long.

Do eagles clean themselves?

Yes. Eagles preen (or clean) themselves so the germs found in the carrion will not get on their bodies. Their long beaks let them eat large prey without getting their heads bloody. This helps eagles spend less time preening their feathers after a meal.

How well can an eagle see?

Eagles can see 8 times better than we can. They can spot a rabbit running from more than 2 miles away. In order for us to see as well as eagles, our eyes would have to be as big as grapefruits. An eagle could even see the buttons on your shirt as it soars (or glides) high above. This is why people call someone "eagle-eyed" if they can see really well.

What kind of nest does an eagle make?

The nest is built with dead wood, vines, and mud. It has grass, feathers, moss, and pine needles on the inside of the nest. An eagle's nest can be as long as a double bed and as tall as a one-story house. A nest in Ohio was used by eagles for 36 years. It weighed 2 tons, or as much as 80 students weighing 50 pounds each! Florida has more nesting Bald Eagles than any other state. January–April is the nesting season in Florida.

How many eggs does an eagle lay?

An eagle's clutch (how many eggs it lays at one time) is usually 2 eggs. They hatch a few days apart. The eggs are dull white. Both parents take turns incubating or sitting on the eggs. It takes about 35 days for the eaglets to hatch. They are ready to fly after about 10 weeks.

What do young eagles look like?

Eaglets are born with fluffy gray feathers. By 6 weeks they are almost as big as their parents, but their eyes and beak are brown. At 8 weeks old they work on making their flight muscles strong. They do this by standing on the nest and flapping their wings. They stay in the nest until they are 10–13 weeks old. They will be fed by their parents for as long as a year.

How big are eagles?

The females are bigger than the males. A female Bald Eagle can weigh 10–14 pounds, and a male can weigh 8–9 pounds. An eagle has over 7,000 feathers. All of those feathers together weigh only 1 pound. The average Bald Eagle is 30–36 inches tall. That is about as tall as an office desk. Their wingspan (from wingtip to wingtip) is about 6–8 feet across—that's taller than most people! An eagle's foot is the size of a human hand. Eagles can live for about 30 years in the wild and up to 50 years in captivity (in a zoo, for example).

How fast can eagles fly?

Eagles can fly 20–40 miles an hour and dive at 100 miles an hour. When eagles catch their prey with their feet, they hold their legs out and fold their wings back. Eagles can soar on air thermals (currents of air) for many hours. These thermals may take them as high as 3 miles above the earth. You may see eagles going in circles or even doing tricks as they fly.

Do eagles ever flock together?

They do not live in flocks. Eagles would rather live in areas of peace and quiet to have their families. They will get together in places where there are other eagles, but each eagle would rather hang out with his or her mate. Eagles mate for life, which means they stay together with their mate until one of them dies. Some eagles migrate (move from one place to another when the seasons change) if they run out of food. When they migrate they move in groups. Sometimes this is called a kettle of eagles. The stream of birds can be 20–30 miles long.

Are Bald Eagles endangered?

No, but the Bald Eagle was endangered at one time. When people cleared land to build houses, the eagles had fewer trees to live in. Also DDT, which was used to kill bugs that were eating the crops, made many animals sick. Now eagles are more likely to die from getting hit by cars. There is something that you can do to help this stop—don't throw food out of your car window. While mice are eating the food, eagles fly down to eat the mice. The eagles can then get hit by cars.

ENDANGERED
SPECIES LIST

BALD EAGLE
KEY DEER
SPOTTED OWL
MANATEE

Make an Eagle's Nest

You will need:
12 oz. of chocolate chips
½ cup of peanut butter (smooth or crunchy)
4 cups of corn flakes
1 cup of chow mein noodles
1–3 yogurt-covered raisins

Melt the chocolate and peanut butter together. Stir in the corn flakes and chow mein noodles. Shape the mixture into a nest. Put it in the freezer to harden. In about 15 minutes add 1–3 "eggs" (yogurt-covered raisins) to complete your nest. Eat it up!

Activities

Make an Edible Eagle

You will need:
1 large white marshmallow
1 chocolate cupcake
1 piece of banana Runts™ candy
2 yellow M&M's™
White icing

Use the icing to stick the marshmallow (head) to an upside down cupcake (chest). Stick one banana piece into the marshmallow for the beak. Add icing on the back of 2 M&M's for the eyes. Use a tiny crumb from the cupcake for the black dot on the eye and stick it on the M&M with icing. Open wide—yum!

Make a Pinecone Eagle

You will need:
A large pinecone
White sheet of paper
White styrofoam ball
2 gold tacks
Yellow pipe cleaner
Yellow foam paper

Fold the paper back and forth like an accordion. Put it in the back of the pinecone. Glue on the styrofoam ball for the head. Add 2 tacks for eyes. Form the pipe cleaner into a triangle and stick it into the ball for the beak. Glue a triangular piece of foam to cover the top of the beak. Use more yellow pipe cleaner to make legs, feet, and claws. Now you have a pinecone eagle to watch over you.

Make a Thumbprint Eagle

You will need:
White, black and yellow paint
Tan paper or shirt

Put your pointer finger in white paint to make the head (vertical). Put your thumb in black paint to make the body. Make one thumbprint, then add another one below it to make the body bigger. For the tail, use the side of your pinky finger. Dip it in white paint each time you make a feather until your tail fan has about 4–5 feathers. Draw a beak and eyes with yellow paint. When it is dry, add a very small black dot on top of the yellow eye.

Where to Learn More about Eagles

Some books about eagles:

Evert, Laura. *Our Wild World Series: Eagles.* Creative Publishing International. 2001.

Hodge, Deborah. *Eagles.* Kids Can Press. 2000.

Landstrom, Lee Ann, and Karen I. Shragg. *Nature's Yucky-Gross Stuff that Helps Nature Work.* Mountain Press Publishing Company. 2003.

Some good eagle websites:

www.carolinaraptorcenter.org

www.enchantedlearning.com

www.seaworld.org

About the Author

Jan Lee Wicker has taught children in pre-kindergarten through first grade for the last 24 years. She currently teaches kindergarten in Weldon, North Carolina, and is pictured with Zlaty from the Carolina Raptor Center. She lives in Roanoke Rapids with her husband and has two grown sons.

If you enjoyed reading this book, here are some other Pineapple Press titles you might enjoy as well. To request our complete catalog or to place an order, write to Pineapple Press, P.O. Box 3889, Sarasota, Florida 34230, or call 1-800-PINEAPL (746-3275). Or visit our website at www.pineapplepress.com.

Those Peculiar Pelicans by Sarah Cussen. Illustrated by Steve Weaver; photographs by Roger Hammond. Find out how much food those peculiar pelicans can fit in their beaks, how they stay cool, whether they really steal fish from fishermen, and more. Ages 5–9.

Those Funny Flamingos by Jan Lee Wicker. Illustrated by Steve Weaver. This is the first of the "Those" series. Learn why those funny flamingos are pink, stand on one leg, eat upside down, and much more. Ages 5–9.

Drawing Florida Wildlife by Frank Lohan. The clearest, easiest method yet for learning to draw Florida's birds, reptiles, amphibians, and mammals. All ages.

Dinosaurs of the South by Judy Cutchins and Ginny Johnston. Dinosaurs lived in the southeastern United States. Loaded with full-color fossil photos as well as art to show what the dinos might have looked like. Ages 8–12.

Ice Age Giants of the South by Judy Cutchins and Ginny Johnston. Learn about the huge animals and reptiles that lived here during the Ice Age. Meet saber-toothed cats, dire wolves, mammoths, giant sloths, and more. Ages 8–12.

Giant Predators of the Ancient Seas by Judy Cutchins and Ginny Johnston. Meet the giant creatures that prowled the waters of prehistory. Ages 8–12.

Florida A to Z by Susan Jane Ryan. Illustrated by Carol Tornatore. From Alligator to Zephyrhills, you'll find out more about Florida packed in this alphabet than you can imagine—200 facts and pictures on Florida history, geography, nature, and people. Ages 8–12.

Florida Lighthouses for Kids by Elinor De Wire. Learn why some lighthouses are tall and some short, why a cat parachuted off St. Augustine Lighthouse, where Florida skeleton and spider lighthouses stand, and much more. Lots of color pictures. Ages 9 and up.

The Young Naturalist's Guide to Florida by Peggy Lantz and Wendy Hale. Where and how to look for Florida's most interesting creatures, including in Florida's special places like the Everglades, coral reefs, sinkholes, salt marshes, and beaches. Ages 10–14.